NEW
TESTAMENT

TIMELESS CHILDREN'S STORIES

AS TOLD BY KARYN HENLEY

ILLUSTRATED BY DENNAS DAVIS

Contents

NEW TESTAMENT TIMELESS CHILDREN'S STORIES

Characters, Topics, & Stories
In The Beginner's Bible™ New Testament

(Page numbers refer to the first page of each story)

Timeless Children's Stories

The New Testament

The Angel's Secret

Gabriel was an angel.
He obeyed God.
Sometimes he took special news
from God to people on earth.

An Angel Visits Mary, *Luke 1*

One day God sent Gabriel to a young lady.
Her name was Mary.
Gabriel went to Mary.
He said, "Greetings!
God is with you!"

Mary was afraid.

She wondered what he meant.

But Gabriel said, "Do not be afraid.

God loves you.

He is going to give you a baby.

You will name him Jesus.

He will be God's Son!"

Mary was surprised.
"How can this be true?" she asked.
"Nothing is impossible with God,"
said Gabriel.

"I believe you," said Mary.
"I will do whatever God wants."
Then Gabriel left Mary.

The Most Special Baby

Now Mary loved a man named Joseph.
They were going to get married.
One day Joseph had to take a trip
to the city of Bethlehem.
So Mary went with him.

The Birth Of Jesus, *Luke 2*

The city of Bethlehem was crowded.

Many people had come there.

Joseph and Mary looked for a place to stay.

But there was no room in any house.

All the beds were full.

People were even sleeping on the floors.

So Joseph and Mary had to stay in a stable

where the donkeys and horses stayed.

That night, the baby was born.
It was God's baby son.
Mary and Joseph named him Jesus,
just as the angel had told them to do.
They wrapped him up so he would be warm.

Mary made a soft bed for him in a manger.
The baby Jesus slept there.
Mary loved him.
Joseph loved him.
And God loved him.

Good News

It was still night.
Outside the town of Bethlehem,
some sheep were sleeping.
Shepherds were watching them.
Suddenly an angel came to the shepherds.
And God's glory shone around them.
They were afraid.

Angels & Shepherds, *Luke 2*

But the angel said, "Do not be afraid.
I am bringing you good news.
This is happy news for all the people:
today in Bethlehem, God's Son was born.
You can go see him.
He is wrapped warm and snug in a manger!"

Then many, many angels came from heaven.
They praised God.
"Glory to God in the highest,
and peace on earth!"

When the angels left, the shepherds said,
"Let's go find this baby!"
So they hurried to town.
They found the stable.
And they saw the new baby.

Then the shepherds left, thanking God.
They told everyone what had happened.
The people were amazed.
And Mary always remembered this special time.

Blessings for the Baby

Soon after Jesus was born,
Joseph and Mary took him to the temple.
There was an old man there named Simeon.
He was waiting to see baby Jesus.
He knew Jesus was special.
He held Jesus in his arms.
He thanked God for baby Jesus.

Simeon & Anna, *Luke 2*

There was also an old woman at the temple.
Her name was Anna.
She also knew Jesus was special.

She came to Mary and Joseph.
She was happy to see baby Jesus.
She, too, thanked God for baby Jesus.

Visitors from the East

God put a special star in the sky
when Jesus was born.
Some wise men who lived in the east
saw this star.
They knew it was a sign.
It meant that a baby king had been born.
These wise men wanted to visit the baby.
So they followed the star for a long way.

The Wise Men Bring Gifts, *Matthew 2*

The wise men went to King Herod in Jerusalem.
"We know a baby king was born," they said.
"Can you tell us where he is?"
This worried the king.
He did not like anyone else
to be called the king.

This is my book.

My name is

L ucas   myerholtz

Will you please read to me?

Thank you.

THE BEGINNERS BIBLE™ NEW TESTAMENT TIMELESS CHILDREN'S STORIES

©1989, 1995, 1997 by James R. Leininger.
All Rights Reserved.
International Copyright Secured.
Printed in the United States of America.

International Standard Book Number: 0-310-92611-4

The Beginners Bible™ trademarks and copyrights are owned by James R. Leininger
and licensed exclusively to Performance Unlimited, Inc. of Brentwood, Tennessee.
The Beginners Bible™ brand of products are produced by Don Wise.

He did not know this baby king
was the king of heaven and earth.
He did not know this baby king was God's Son.
"I do not know this new king,"
said King Herod.
"But go and find him.
Then tell me where he is."

So the wise men went on.
And the star led them right to the place
where Jesus was.
They were very happy they had found him.
They bowed down.
They gave him gifts: sweet-smelling gifts,
sparkling, golden gifts.

God knew King Herod did not like
anyone else to be called the king.
God sent the wise men a dream.
This dream told them not to tell King Herod
where the baby was.
So the wise men went home a different way.

Running Away

The wise men did not go back to King Herod.
King Herod was upset.
He wanted to find the baby king.
He wanted to kill him.
Herod wanted to be the only king around.

Escape From King Herod, *Matthew 2*

But God knew what King Herod was thinking.
God sent an angel to Joseph in a dream.
The angel said, "Run away to Egypt.
Stay there until I say you can come back."

So Joseph and Mary and baby Jesus
went to Egypt.
They lived there until King Herod died.
Then an angel came again to Joseph.
"You can move back home," he said.
"It is safe now."

Joseph took Mary and Jesus back.
They moved to the town of Nazareth.
Jesus grew up in Nazareth.
God made him strong and wise.

The Man Who Could Not Talk

Zechariah worked in God's temple.

He loved God.

His wife Elizabeth loved God.

They were very old.

But they had no children.

Zechariah & Elizabeth, *Luke 1*

One day at the temple,
an angel came to Zechariah.
The angel said, "I am Gabriel.
I have good news.
You and Elizabeth will have a baby.
You will call him John.
He will be filled with God's Holy Spirit.
He will be a special man."

Zechariah said, "How do I know this is true?"
"You will not be able to speak
until all of this happens," said Gabriel.
"Then you will know that this is true."

When Zechariah came out of the temple,
he could not talk.
He could only move his hands
to tell what he wanted to say.

It all happened as the angel said.
Zechariah and Elizabeth did have a baby.
Everyone wanted to name him Zechariah
like his father.
But Zechariah shook his head.
He remembered what the angel told him.
He wrote on a tablet: "His name is John."
Then God made him able to talk again.
And Zechariah praised God.

Lost!

Jesus grew up in Nazareth.
When Jesus was 12 years old,
Mary and Joseph took him to the temple.
The temple was in Jerusalem.
They had to travel there by walking.
They went with many of their friends
and family.

Young Jesus In The Temple, *Luke 2*

There were many people in Jerusalem.
It was crowded.
Jesus had a good time there
with friends and family.
But when it was time to go home,
Jesus stayed in Jerusalem.

Mary and Joseph thought he was walking
with his friends.
That night, they looked for him.
When they could not find him,
they were worried.
Jesus was lost!
They hurried back to Jerusalem.

For three days they hunted for Jesus.
At last they found him.
He was in the temple.
He was listening to the wise teachers there.
And he was asking them questions.

Mary said, "We have been worried about you."
Jesus said, "I had to come
to my Father's house."
Jesus knew that God was his Father.
He had been talking to the teachers about God.
But he went home with Mary and Joseph.
And he obeyed them.
God blessed Jesus, and he grew wise and strong.

In the Jordan River

Zechariah and Elizabeth's baby John grew up.
He lived in the desert.
His clothes were made of camel's hair.
He wore a leather belt.
And he ate locusts and wild honey.
He told the people about God.
He also told them that a special man
would come soon: Jesus, the Son of God.

John Baptizes Jesus, *Luke 3*

Many people listened to John.
John told them to stop doing bad
and to start doing good.

He baptized people in the Jordan River.
He dipped them quickly under the water.
This showed everyone that they
wanted to follow God.
They wanted to stop being bad.
They wanted to start being good.

One day Jesus came to the river.
Jesus asked John to baptize him.
John knew Jesus was the Son of God.
John said, "You are greater than I am.
You should baptize me."
But Jesus said, "No.
I want to do everything that is right."
So John baptized Jesus.

As soon as Jesus came up out of the water,
the Spirit of God came down from heaven.
It looked like a dove.
It landed on Jesus.
And God said, "This is my Son.
I love him.
I am pleased with him."

Helpers and Friends

Jesus knew that he had much work to do.
He wanted to have some good friends
who could help him.
One day Jesus was walking
by the Sea of Galilee.
He saw two boats there.
Peter and Andrew were fishing from one boat.
James and John were mending a net
in the other boat.
Jesus called to them, "Come and follow me."
And they did.

Calling The Disciples, *Luke 5 & 6*

Later, Jesus passed by a tax office.
There was a man there named Matthew.
Matthew's job was to take the taxes,
the money the people paid to the king.
Jesus looked at Matthew.
"Follow me," Jesus said.
Matthew got up and followed Jesus.

Jesus asked twelve men to be his helpers.
Besides Peter, Andrew, James, John and
Matthew, he called Philip, Bartholomew,
Thomas, another man named James,
Simon, Thaddaeus and Judas.

A Wedding Party

One day, Jesus and his helper friends
went to a wedding party.
It was a happy time for everyone.
There was food to eat and wine to drink.

Water Into Wine, *John 2*

But Jesus' mother came over to him.

"Something terrible has happened," she said.

"They have run out of wine!"

Then she looked at the servants.

"Do whatever Jesus tells you," she said.

There were six very big stone jars nearby.
Jesus told the servants, "Fill those jars
with water."
So the servants filled the jars to the top.
"Now dip some out," said Jesus.
"Give it to the people."

The servants dipped out the water.
But it was not water anymore!
It was wine!

The people drank it.
Some of them said it was the best wine
at the party.
They did not know it had been
plain water.
But the servants knew.
God had given Jesus special power,
because Jesus was God's Son.

Through the Roof

Crowds of people went to see Jesus.
They listened to him teach.
He even healed the sick people.
One day, Jesus was teaching inside a house.
So many people came to see him,
that the house was full.

Jesus Heals A Paralytic, *Mark 2 & Luke 5*

Four men came with their friend.
Their friend could not walk.
They had to carry him on a little bed.
But they could not get to Jesus.
The house was too full.

That did not stop them.
There were some stairs outside the house.
Up the stairs they went to the roof.
They took off some tiles of the roof
and made a hole.
Then they let their friend down
right through the roof,
right in front of Jesus.

When Jesus saw the man,
he said, "Get up and walk."
The man stood up.
He walked home praising God.
Everybody else was amazed.
They thanked God, too.

On a Mountain

Old men went to see Jesus.
Children went to see Jesus.
Young men and women,
mothers and fathers went to see Jesus.

Sermon On The Mount, *Matthew 5 & 6*

Happy people, sad people, well people,
sick people went to see Jesus.
They wanted to hear what Jesus said.

Jesus saw the people coming.
So he went up the side of a mountain.
He sat down.
"Look at the birds," he said.
"Do they have barns
where they keep their food?
No, God feeds them."

"And look at the flowers.
They do not work.
They do not make clothes to wear.
God dresses them in clothes
more beautiful than a king's."

"You are more important than birds.
You are more important than flowers.
So do not worry.
If God takes care of them,
he will take care of you."

A Sick Servant

There was once a captain in an army.
Many men had to obey him,
because he was in charge.
He was the boss.
Now there was one man
who was very special to the captain.
This man was his helper, his servant.

The Centurion, *Luke 7*

One day the servant got very sick.

He could not move.

He was hurting.

The captain was sad to see his servant sick.

But the captain knew about Jesus.

He knew that Jesus could make people well.

So the captain found Jesus.

"Lord," he said, "My servant is sick.

He is hurting."

Jesus said, "I will go and make him well."

But the captain said,
"You do not have to come.
Just say the word and my servant will be well.
I know, because I am in charge of many men.
They do what I tell them to do.
You are in charge of this sickness.
It will do what you tell it to do."

Jesus was amazed, because the captain
knew that Jesus had such power.
The captain believed.
"Go back home," Jesus said.
"Your servant will be well."
The captain went home.
And, just as Jesus had said,
his servant *was* well!

The Farmer's Seeds

Jesus liked to tell the people stories.
His stories had special meanings.
One day, he told this story.
"Once there was a farmer.
He went to his field to plant his seeds.
He scattered the seeds here and there.

Parables Told By Jesus, *Matthew 13*

Now some of the seeds fell on the path.
The birds flew down and ate those seeds.
Some of the seeds fell in rocky dirt.
They sprouted, but there were too many rocks.
The roots could not grow and get water.
So when the sun grew hot on them, they died.

Some seeds fell where there were weeds.
The seeds sprouted, but the weeds grew bigger
and crowded them out.
Other seeds fell into good dirt.
There were no weeds or rocks.
They settled deep into the dirt
where no birds could get them.
And they grew and grew and grew."

The people wondered about this story.
"What does it mean?" they asked Jesus.
And Jesus told them.
"The seed is the news about God.
The birds and weeds and rocks
are like some people's hearts.
They hear God's word,
but they have their hearts on other things.

They do not understand.
They do not love God and follow him.
But the good dirt is like the hearts
of people who do understand.
They love God.
God's love grows in their hearts
like a beautiful, healthy plant."

A Tiny Seed and a Big Tree

Many people came to hear Jesus' stories.
Jesus told stories about God's kingdom.
God's kingdom is wherever God is king.
And wherever God is king,
his love will be found.

Parables Told By Jesus, *Matthew 13*

Jesus said God's kingdom is like
a mustard seed.
It is one of the smallest seeds in the world.
But it grows and grows and grows!
And when it is grown, it is one of the
biggest plants in the garden.
It is so big that birds come and rest on its
branches.

God's kingdom can start very small.
God's love may be in only one person's heart.
But when his love is shared,
his kingdom grows and grows and grows!
More and more people want to follow God.

Jesus told another story.

He said God's kingdom is like yeast.

Bakers use yeast to make dough puff up.

Then it will make soft, fluffy
loaves of bread.

Jesus said God's kingdom is like yeast.

A woman mixed the yeast with flour.

She made dough.

The yeast made the dough grow big and puffy.

God's love can start small like yeast.
It can mix into our hearts.
There it grows bigger and bigger.
Soon we have enough love to share
with everyone.

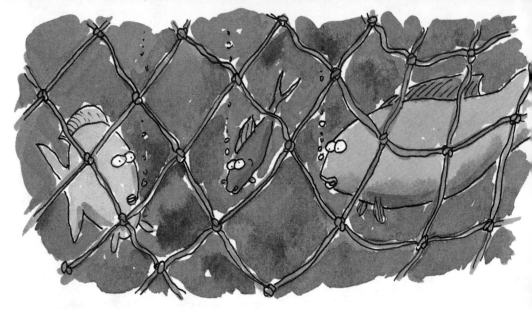

The Net

"Once there was a fisherman," said Jesus.
"He threw out his net.
Down, down it went into the lake.
Soon the fish began to swim around the net.
Many fish swam into the net.
The fisherman waited and watched.
When the net was full,
he pulled it up onto the shore.

Parables Told By Jesus, *Matthew 13*

"Then he sat down and sorted the fish.
He tossed the good fish into the baskets.
But he threw the bad fish away."

"God's kingdom is like the net," said Jesus.
"Many people will come to it.
One day the angels will sort the people.
The good people will get to stay
in God's kingdom, but the bad people will not."

The Treasure and the Pearl

"God's kingdom is like a treasure," said Jesus.

It is like a treasure hidden in a field.

A man was working in the field.

He did not know about the treasure.

Tap, tap.

His shovel bumped something.

He looked at it.

He dusted it off.

Parables Told By Jesus, *Matthew 13*

It was real treasure!
He was so excited!
He quickly hid the treasure again.
Then he sold everything he had.
He took the money and bought the field.
Then he ran back and dug up the treasure.

"God's kingdom is like a man who
buys and sells," said Jesus.
This man looks for good things
people would like to buy.
He gets those things and sells them to people.
One day this man was looking for pearls.
He looked and looked.
Then he saw it!

It was a perfect, beautiful pearl!

And it cost a lot of money.

But the man did not care.

He sold everything else he had.

He took the money and bought the pearl.

God's kingdom is the real treasure.

God's kingdom is perfect like the pearl.

It is better than anything else in the world.

It is worth anything you might give up for it.

Wind and Waves

It was late in the day.
Jesus was teaching by the lake.
Many people had come to see him.
And Jesus was tired.
"Let's go to the other side
of the lake," he said to his friends.

Jesus Calms The Storm, *Matthew 8, Mark 4, & Luke 8*

So they got into their boat.
They started to sail across the lake.
The boat rocked gently up and down.

But the wind began to blow stronger.
The waves began to crash into the boat.
It bobbed high and then dipped low.
Water sloshed into the boat!
Everyone was afraid.
Everyone but Jesus.

Jesus was asleep on a pillow
in the back of the boat.
His friends woke him up.
"Jesus! Don't you hear the wind howling?
Can't you feel the boat tossing?
We are all going to drown!"
"Why are you afraid?" Jesus asked.

Then he looked at the wind and the stormy sea.

"Peace!" he said. "Be still."

The wind stopped blowing.

The waves stopped crashing.

Everything was quiet and still.

Jesus' friends were amazed.

"Even the wind and the waves obey Jesus,"

they said.

One Touch

People crowded around Jesus as he walked.
They pushed this way and that.
They even bumped into Jesus.
Some people just wanted to see
what Jesus looked like.
Some wanted to talk to him.
Some wanted to listen to him.

A Woman Touches Jesus, *Mark 5 & Luke 8*

One woman wanted Jesus to make her well.
She had been sick for twelve years.
She had spent all her money
going to see doctors.
No one could make her better.
She kept thinking, "If I could only
get to Jesus!
If I could just touch his clothes!"

She pushed closer and closer.
Finally she was close enough.
She reached out—she touched his cloak!
Right away she felt better!
She knew she was well!

Jesus stopped walking.
He turned around.
"Who touched me?" he asked.
"All these people are crowding around you,"
Peter said.
"Many people touched you."
"But I felt some power go out of me,"
Jesus said.

Then the woman came to Jesus.

"I touched you," she said.

"And you are well now, because you believed,"
said Jesus.

"Go in peace."

A Big Picnic

More than 10 people,
more than 50 people,
more than 100 people,
more than 1,000 people,
5,000 people had come to hear Jesus.
They stayed all afternoon.
At dinnertime, they were still listening
to Jesus.

Jesus Feeds The Five Thousand, *Matthew 14, Mark 6, & Luke 9*

118

Jesus' friends said, "Let's tell
these people to leave now.
They can go and get something to eat."
"They do not need to go," said Jesus.
"But we do not have the money
to buy food for them," said Philip.

"You are right," said Andrew.
"And I only know one person who brought food.
A little boy here has five loaves of bread
and two fish.
That is not enough to feed 5,000 people!"

But Jesus said, "Tell the people to sit down."
Everyone sat down on the soft grass.
Jesus took the five loaves and the two fish.
He prayed and thanked God for the food.
Then his friends began to give food
to the people.

Now, there were not only five loaves
and two fish.
There was plenty of bread and fish
for everyone.
Each person got to eat as much as he wanted.

Walking on Water

Night was coming.
Jesus was tired.
It had been a very busy day.
Jesus wanted to be alone for awhile.
He wanted to pray.
While he went up into the hills,
his friends got into their boat.
They started rowing to the other side
of the lake.

Jesus Walks On Water, *Matthew 14*

The wind was blowing against them.
It pushed their boat back.
Jesus saw that they were having
a hard time rowing.
So he came to them walking on the water!
When they saw him, they were scared.
They did not know it was Jesus.

Jesus knew they were scared.
"Do not be afraid," he said, "It is I."
Peter wanted to make sure this was true.
"If it really is you," he said,
"tell me to come to you on the water."
"Come on," said Jesus.

Peter got out of the boat.

Step, step, step.

He began to walk on the water, too!

But then he felt the strong wind.

He looked at the waves.

He began to sink.

"Jesus, save me!" he cried.

Right away, Jesus pulled Peter up.

"Why did you get scared?" Jesus asked.

Then they climbed into the boat.

The wind stopped blowing.

Everyone worshipped Jesus.

"You really *are* God's Son," they said.

Open Eyes

He could not see flowers.
He could not see people.
He could not see anything.
He had been blind ever since he was born.
But something special happened
to this blind man:
Jesus saw him.

Jesus Heals A Blind Man, *John 9*

129

Jesus did something strange.
He spit on the dirt and made some mud.
Then he put the mud on the man's eyes.
"Go and wash your eyes," Jesus said.

The man did what Jesus said.

He washed the mud off his eyes.

He looked around.

He could see!

And the man worshipped Jesus.

Money in a Fish

In the land where Jesus lived,
everyone had to pay money to their king.
This money was called the tax.
The men who took the money
were called tax collectors.

Jesus & The Tax, *Matthew 17*

One day the tax collectors came to Peter.
"Does Jesus pay the tax money?" they asked.
"Yes," Peter answered, "he does."
Then he went to find Jesus.

But Jesus already knew
about the tax collectors.
He knew what to do.
"Go fishing at the lake," said Jesus.
"When you catch your first fish,
look in its mouth."

So Peter went fishing.
He looked into the mouth of his first fish.
Inside its mouth, he found some money!
He took that money to the tax collectors.
There was plenty to pay Jesus' tax
and Peter's tax.

A Good Neighbor

"I know that I should love God,"
a man once said to Jesus.
"I should love him with all my heart.
And I should love my neighbor, too.
But who is my neighbor?"
Jesus told him this story.

The Good Samaritan, *Luke 10*

There was a man walking along a road.

He was going on a trip.

Suddenly, robbers jumped out at him.

They hit him.

They took all the things he had with him.

And they left him, hurt, lying by the road.

A short time later, step, step, step,
someone came down the road.
It was a man who worked in God's temple.
He could help the hurt man!
But, no, when he saw the hurt man,
he crossed the road.
He passed by on the other side!
Soon another man came.
But he passed by, too.

Then, clop, clop, clip, clop,
along came a man on a donkey.
This was a man from a different country.
When he saw the hurt man, he stopped.
He put bandages on his hurt places.
And he took the man to a house
where he could rest and get well.

Jesus finished his story.
He looked at the man.
"Who was a neighbor to the hurt man?"
Jesus asked.
"The one who helped him," said the man.
"Then you can be a neighbor to anyone
who needs your help," said Jesus.

Listening

Once there were two sisters.

One was named Mary.

One was named Martha.

Jesus was their good friend.

He came to see them whenever he was in town.

Mary & Martha, *Luke 10*

One time while Jesus was at their house,
he had a long talk with Mary.
Mary sat by Jesus.
She listened and listened.
Jesus had so many wonderful things to say.

Martha was thinking about other things.

She knew there was a lot of work to do.

She wanted to get their dinner ready.

She wanted to clean the house.

She wanted to make a nice bed for Jesus.

And while Martha worked, worked, worked,

Mary sat and listened.

Finally Martha got upset.
"Jesus," she said, "Mary is not helping.
I am doing all this work by myself.
Tell her to come and help me!"

"Martha, Martha," Jesus said.

"You are upset about so many things.

Mary is doing something very important.

She is listening to me.

She chose to do the best thing."

The Woman Who Could Not Stand Up

Saturdays were special days for God's people.
They called Saturday the Sabbath.
God had said it was a day for resting.
And it was a day the people worshipped God.
Some of the leaders of God's people
made up rules for the Sabbath.
"There are six days for work," they said.
"You must not do *any* work on the Sabbath."

The Crippled Woman, *Luke 13*

One Sabbath, Jesus was teaching the people.
A crippled woman was there.
She was bent over.
She could not stand up straight.

When Jesus saw her, he told her
to come to him.
Then he said to her, "You are now made well."
He put his hands on her.
Right away she stood straight and tall.
And she praised God.

The leaders were angry.
They said, "Jesus, you worked when you
made this woman well.
You worked on the Sabbath day!"

But Jesus said, "You take your donkey
and your ox to get water on the Sabbath day.
That is work, too.
If you can do that kind of work,
then I can heal this woman."
They knew Jesus was right.
And all the people were excited about
the wonderful things Jesus was doing.

The Lost Sheep

Jesus liked to tell stories
that had special meanings.
One time he told this story.

"Pretend you are a shepherd," Jesus said.
"You have 100 sheep.
You take good care of them.
You show them where the sweetest grass is.
You show them where the coolest water is.
You know each one of your sheep.
And you love them all.

The Sheep, *Luke 15*

155

Every night as you take them to their pen,
you count your sheep.
You want to be sure they are all there,
safe and sound.
When you count '100,'
you know they are all there.
You close the gate and the sheep sleep safely.

But one night, you are counting . . .
95, 96, 97, 98, 99 . . . 99?
Only 99 sheep?
You count again, but there are only 99 sheep.
The other sheep must be lost!
Do you say, 'Oh well, at least I have 99 sheep?'
No, you go to find that lost sheep.

You look and look and look.
and when at last you find it,
you carry it home on your shoulders.
You are so happy that you call your friends.
'Look,' you say, 'I found my lost sheep!'"

Then Jesus told the special meaning
of this story.
"God is like the shepherd," he said.
"God loves his people.
If one of them disobeys him,
he's like the lost sheep.
But when he is sorry and comes back to God,
God is happy.
God is like a shepherd who has found
his lost sheep!"

The Lost Coin

"Once there was a woman who had
ten silver coins," said Jesus.
"Sometimes she would count them.
One, two, three, four, five, six,
seven, eight, nine, ten . . . ten coins.
One day something was wrong.
One, two, three, four, five, six,
seven, eight, nine . . . nine?
Only nine?
Where could the other coin be?

The Coin, *Luke 15*

She lit her lamp so she could see
under the furniture.
She even swept her house looking for the coin.
Suddenly she saw it!
She picked it up and called her friends.
'Be happy with me,' she said.
'I have found my lost coin.'"

God is like that woman.
He wants to find his people
who are not following him.
They are lost from him.
He wants them to follow him again.
Then they will be found,
and God will be happy!

The Lost Son

"There was once a man who had two sons,"
said Jesus.
"The younger son was not happy at home.
He dreamed of an exciting life far away.
One day, he decided to leave his home.
So he went to his dad.
'I know that part of your land is mine,'
he said.
'I want you to pay me for my share.'

The Son, *Luke 15*

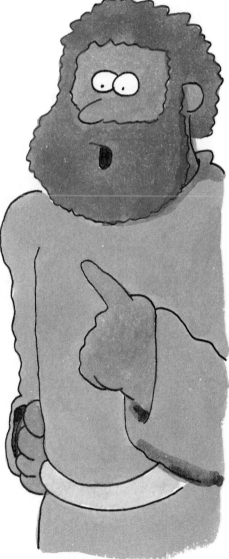

The father gave the son what he wanted.

The son took it all and went far away.

At first he was happy.

He did whatever he wanted to do.

He went wherever he wanted to go.

He bought whatever he wanted to buy.

Before long he spent all his money.

He did not even have the money to buy food.

So he got a job feeding pigs.

He was sad.

He wanted to go home.

He was also afraid.

Maybe his father would not like him anymore.

But he began the long trip home.

At least he could be a servant instead of a son.

His father saw him coming.
He ran to meet him.
He hugged and kissed him.
'Let's have a party,' he said.
'My son was lost, but now he is found!'"
God is like this father.
He is full of joy when someone decides
to obey him.

The Man Who Remembered

Ten men were very sad.
They were sad, because they were sick.
They were so sick, they had to
live away from their families.
They had to live away from their friends.

Jesus Heals The Lepers, *Luke 17*

One day the ten men found out
that Jesus was coming their way.
They decided to go meet him.
When they saw him, they called, "Jesus, Jesus!"
Jesus looked.
And he said, "Go to the priest.
Let him take a look at you."

Now the priest was the one
who could tell them if they were well.
He could tell them if they could
live with their families again.
So they started on their way to see the priest.

While the men were walking,
they began to notice something.
They were feeling better.
They were looking better.
In fact, they were all well!

They were so excited.

They hurried on to see the priest.

All but one.

One man remembered something.

He remembered to go back to Jesus
and say thank you.

The Children

Mothers held their babies as they walked.
Boys and girls skipped and hopped
down the road.
They were happy.
They were going to see Jesus.

Jesus Loves The Children, *Matthew 19, Mark 10, & Luke 18*

175

But when they got to the place
where Jesus was, Jesus' friends told them
to go away.
"You cannot come to see Jesus," they said.
"He is too busy for children.
He has important things to do."

Now Jesus found out
what his friends were saying.
He was angry.
"Do not stop the children," he said.
"Let them come to me."

So they came:
little boys and little girls,
and even babies.
They came to Jesus.
And Jesus took them in his arms.

He was not too busy.

He held them.

He blessed them.

He loved them.

Children are important to Jesus.

The Blind Beggar

His name was Bartimaeus.
And he could not see.
He could not work like other men did
to get money to buy food.
So every day, he sat beside the road.
He asked the people who passed by
to give him money.

Bartimaeus, *Mark 10*

One day he heard a lot of people passing by.

"There are so many people," he said.

"What's going on?"

"Jesus is coming," they told him.

Right away Bartimaeus began calling, "Jesus!"
The people turned to Bartimaeus.
"Shhhh!" they said. "Be quiet!"
But he shouted even louder, "Jesus! Jesus!"

Jesus heard Bartimaeus.

He stopped.

"What do you want me to do for you?" he asked.

"Oh, Jesus," said Bartimaeus.

"Please make my eyes see!"

Then Jesus said, "Your eyes may see,
because you believed."
All of a sudden, Bartimaeus could see!
He could see all the colors and shapes.
He could see all the people.
He could see Jesus.
He praised God.
All the people praised God, too.

A Small Man

Zacchaeus was a man who took tax money
from people.
Tax money was what they had to pay
to their king.
But Zacchaeus took more money
than he was supposed to.
He kept it to make himself rich.
And nobody liked him.

Zacchaeus, *Luke 19*

One day, Jesus was passing by his town.

Everyone went to see Jesus.

Even Zacchaeus went to see Jesus.

But Zacchaeus had a problem.

He was short.

Everyone was in his way.

He could not see.

Then Zacchaeus had an idea.

He ran ahead of all the people.

He climbed a tall tree.

He had found the perfect place to watch Jesus.

He could see all the people coming.

When Jesus got to the tree, he stopped.
He looked up at Zacchaeus.
"Zacchaeus," he said, "come down right away.
I need to stay at your house today!"

Zacchaeus scrambled down that tree.

Jesus wanted to stay with him!

He took Jesus to his house.

He told Jesus, "I want to do what is right.

I will give back the money I took

to make me rich."

Jesus was pleased.

Zacchaeus had chosen to do the right thing.

Two Small Coins

The temple was big and beautiful.
Many people came there to worship God.
Inside the temple were some big money boxes.
They were open at the top,
so the people could put money in them.
The money was for the temple
and all that was used in worship to God.

The Widow's Coins, *Mark 12 & Luke 21*

One day Jesus sat down across from
the money boxes.
He saw many rich people put in lots of money.
Then one poor woman walked up to the boxes.
She put in two small coins.

Jesus looked at his friends.
"This poor woman put in more
than the rich people did," he said.
"Here's why: the rich people
still have much money left.
But this woman only had two coins.
She did not have any more money.
The rich people only gave part
of what they had.
She gave all of what she had."

The Man at the Pool

There was once a very special pool.
The water was calm most of the time.
But sometimes it bubbled and bubbled.
Sick people came to this pool.
When the water bubbled,
they got into the pool.
Then they would feel well.

Jesus Heals The Man At The Pool, *John 5*

One day Jesus was walking by the pool.
There he saw a man who could not walk.
The man had been lame for a long time.
So Jesus asked the man,
"Do you want to get well?"

"Oh, yes, I do," said the man.
"But I do not know anyone who will help me
get into the pool when the water bubbles."
Then Jesus said, "Get up.
Pick up your mat and walk."

Right away the man's legs were well.
He stood up and he walked!
The leaders of the people were angry,
because it was the Sabbath day.
They thought the man should not carry
his mat on the Sabbath.
But Jesus said, "God is always working,
even today.
So I am working, too."

Mary's Gift

Mary and Martha were two
of Jesus' good friends.
They were getting ready
for a big dinner party at their house.
It was a dinner for Jesus.
They had invited all his good friends.

The Perfume, *John 12*

That night many people sat down
together at Mary and Martha's table.
Martha was busy as always.
She carried the food to the table.

But Mary did a surprising thing.
She took some perfume that cost
a lot of money.
She poured it on Jesus' feet.
Then she wiped his feet with her hair.
Mmmm! It made the whole house smell sweet!

One of Jesus' friends was named Judas.
He said, "Why didn't Mary sell this perfume?
She could give us the money.
Then we could give it to the poor people."
But Judas said this because *he* really
wanted the money.
He was the keeper of the money bag.
He took money out of the bag
when no one was looking.
He spent the money on himself.

"Leave Mary alone," said Jesus.
"She gave this perfume to me as a gift,
because I will not always be able
to be here with you."

Make Way for the King

Two of Jesus' friends went
to look for a donkey.
Jesus had told them just where to find it.
It would be tied right by the village gate.
It was going to be a special donkey.
Jesus was going to ride on it.

Here Comes The King, *John 12*

When the friends found the donkey,
they took it to Jesus.
They put their coats on its back,
and Jesus got on.

When the people saw Jesus coming,
they began to shout with joy.
"Hosanna! Hosanna!
Blessed is the King who comes
in the name of the Lord!"

Some people cut branches off the palm trees.
They laid the branches on the road.
Other people spread their coats on the road.
And they all praised God in loud voices
for the wonderful things Jesus had done.

Jesus rode to the big city of Jerusalem.

The crowds followed him.

The leaders of the people were angry.

"See how all the people follow Jesus now?

They do not follow us anymore.

We must get rid of Jesus," they said.

Washing Feet

Jesus knew that not everyone liked him.
He knew the leaders were angry with him.
In fact, they were so angry and so jealous,
they wanted to kill him.
And Jesus knew that, too.

Jesus Washes The Disciples' Feet, *John 13*

But Jesus still had his special friends:
Peter, Andrew, James, John, Philip,
Bartholomew, Simon, Matthew, James,
Thomas, Thaddaeus and Judas.
They had been his friends for a long time.
They traveled with Jesus.
And Jesus taught them many things.

One night, they all got together for dinner.
While they were eating, Jesus got up.
He put a towel on like an apron.
He poured water into a large bowl.
Then he began to wash his friends' feet.

When Jesus got to Peter's feet,
Peter said, "I cannot let you wash my feet."
"If you don't let me wash your feet,
you can't follow me," said Jesus.
"In that case," said Peter, "wash my hands
and my head, too!"

After Jesus washed his friends' feet,
he asked, "Do you understand what I did?
I showed you how to be kind to each other.
I am your Lord and Teacher.
If I can be kind and help you,
then you can be kind and help each other."

The Last Supper

Judas, one of Jesus' friends, had a bad idea.
He knew that the leaders were angry with Jesus.
He knew they wanted to catch Jesus.
Now Judas wanted money more than anything.
So he told the leaders that he would
show them where Jesus was if they would
pay him some money.
They paid him 30 pieces of silver.

The Upper Room, *Matthew 26*

One night, Jesus and his friends
were eating supper together.
"One of you is planning to do something
bad to me," Jesus said.
"Who is it?" asked John.

Jesus said, "It is the one I give bread to."
Then he gave a piece of bread to Judas.
"Go on," Jesus told him.
"Do what you are planning to do."
Judas got up and left.
Only Judas and Jesus knew
what Judas' bad idea was.

Then Jesus gave thanks, and broke some bread.
He shared it with his friends.
Next he took a cup of wine and gave thanks.
He shared this with his friends, too.
"Whenever you eat the bread and drink
the wine, remember me," he said.

Then Jesus said, "I will not be
with you much longer.
I have to leave.
But do not worry.
Do not be afraid.
I will come back.
You are my friends.
Love each other as I love you."

Sadness

It was night.

Jesus took his friends to a garden.

There Jesus prayed.

And there Judas carried out his bad idea.

He led soldiers to the garden.

He showed them where Jesus was.

Jesus knew he would.

And it was all right.

Jesus went with them.

The Crucifixion, *John 18 & 19*

You see, it was time for Jesus to die.
God had planned it long ago.
Jesus knew it would happen
when he came to the earth.
He came to take the punishment
for all the wrong things anybody
had ever done, or ever would do.
And now it was time.
The soldiers took him to the leaders.

The leaders did not believe he was God's Son.
They said, "He must die, because
he calls himself the Son of God."
So they killed him on a cross.
It was a sad day for Jesus' friends.
But they did not know that God had planned
a wonderful surprise for them.
And they would not be sad for long!

Surprise!

After Jesus died, a rich man named Joseph
took Jesus' body.
He put it in a special cave-tomb.
He rolled a huge stone
over the opening of the cave.
The leaders sent guards to watch the cave
to make sure no one took Jesus' body.

The Resurrection, *Matthew 27 & 28*

But early Sunday morning,
there was an earthquake.
An angel came from heaven
and rolled the stone away.
When the guards saw him,
they shook with fear and fell down.

One of Jesus' friends named Mary
came to the cave-tomb early that morning.
She saw the stone was not in front of it,
so she went in.
She saw an angel there.
"Jesus is not here," the angel said.
"He is alive!
Go tell his friends that they will get to
see him again!"

Mary was not sad anymore.
Jesus was not dead.
He was alive!
She ran back to tell the wonderful news.
At first, Jesus' friends did not believe her.
But she was right!
Jesus did come back to see them.
He really *was* alive!

Fish for Breakfast

Late one day, Peter, James and John,
and some of Jesus' other friends
were together by the Sea of Galilee.
"I'm going fishing," said Peter.
"We will go with you," said the others.

Jesus Has Risen, *John 21*

They sailed out in their boat.
They threw their net into the water.
And they waited and waited and waited.
All night they fished,
but they did not catch anything.

Early in the morning, they saw someone
standing on the shore.
He called, "Have you caught any fish?"
"No," they yelled.
"Throw your net on the other side
of the boat," the man called.
So they threw the net on the other side.

All at once, fish filled the net.
John looked at Peter.
"It's Jesus!" he said.
Peter was so excited,
he jumped into the water.
He swam to the shore.

It *was* Jesus!

He made a little campfire.

He cooked fish and bread on it.

"Come and have some breakfast," Jesus called.

They did not have to ask who he was.

They knew he was their best friend Jesus.

He was alive!

Jesus Goes Home

Jesus led his friends to a place near Bethany.
He lifted his hands up and blessed them.
"Tell other people about me," he said.
Then he went up into the sky.
A cloud hid him,
so his friends could not see him.
They stood looking up into the sky
for a long time.

Jesus Goes To Heaven, *Matthew 28 & Acts 1*

All of a sudden, two angels stood beside them.
"Why are you still looking into the sky?"
the angels asked.
"Jesus has gone up to heaven.
Someday he will come back
the same way you saw him leave."
Then the friends went back to the city
with joy in their hearts.

Jesus had taught them many things.
They would always remember that he said,
"Do not worry or be afraid.
Trust in God and trust in me.
In God's house there are many rooms.
I will go to make a place ready for you.
Someday I will come back and take you
with me so you can be where I am."

Wind and Fire

Before Jesus went home to be with God,
he told his friends to stay in Jerusalem.
He said they would get a gift there.
So they waited in Jerusalem.

Pentecost, *Acts 2*

Now there was a great holiday coming
called Pentecost.
Many people came to Jerusalem
from far and near to celebrate that day.
The friends of Jesus celebrated, too.

Suddenly they heard a sound
like a strong wind blowing.
And they saw something that looked like
little flames of fire resting on them.
Then God's Holy Spirit filled them.
This was the gift Jesus had told them
to wait for!

They began to speak in languages
they did not know.
The people who were there from other
countries heard Jesus' friends speaking.
And they could understand them.
The languages Jesus' friends were speaking
were the same languages they spoke.
The people were amazed!

"This is what God promised us," Peter said.
Then he told them about Jesus.
Many people believed in Jesus that day.

Peter and John and the Beggar

There once was a man who could not walk.
Every day he sat at the gate to the temple.
He begged people to give him some money
so he could buy food and clothes.

Jesus Heals The Beggar, *Acts 3*

One afternoon, Peter and John went
to the temple.
The beggar man saw them.
He asked them for some money.
When Peter and John looked at him,
he thought they were going to give him money.

"We do not have any silver or gold,"
said Peter.
"But we will be glad to give you
what we have.
In the name of Jesus, walk."
Peter took the man by the hand
and helped him up.

Right away, the man's feet grew strong.
He walked.
He jumped.
He went into the temple praising God.

When the people saw him, they were amazed.
"It is Jesus' power
that has made this man well," said Peter.
Then all the people began to praise God,
because the lame man could walk.

A Bright Light

There was once a very mean man named Saul.
He did not like anyone who loved Jesus.
He wanted to catch them and put them in jail.
He traveled near and far to find them.
One of his trips took him
to the big city of Damascus.

Saul's Conversion, *Acts 9*

While he was on his way,
a bright light suddenly flashed from the sky.
It shone all around Saul.
Saul closed his eyes.
A voice called, "Saul, Saul,
why are you doing these mean things?"
Saul was scared!

"Who are you?" Saul asked.

"I am Jesus," said the voice.

"Now get up and go to the city.
There you will find out what to do."

Saul got up.

But when he opened his eyes, he could not see.

His friends had to lead him to the city.

In that city lived a good man named Ananias.
Jesus came to him in a dream and said,
"Go find Saul."
So Ananias went to Saul.
He touched Saul and said,
"Jesus sent me so you could see again.
Jesus wants you to be one of his friends."

Right away, Saul could see again.
He got up and was baptized.
And he was not mean anymore.
He even changed his name.
Now everyone called him Paul.
And for the rest of his life,
Paul told others about Jesus.

Paul and Silas in Jail

Paul had a very good friend named Silas.
They went near and far telling about Jesus.
Many people believed
and became followers of Jesus.
They were called Christians.
But some people did not believe.
They did not like Christians.

The Jailer, *Acts 16*

In one town, these men
put Paul and Silas in jail.
But Paul and Silas did not worry.
They knew God was with them everywhere.
Even in jail!
They sang and prayed in jail.

The other people in jail listened.
About midnight, there was an earthquake.
The chains on the prisoners fell off!
All the jail doors flew open!
The jailer woke up and ran into the jail.
He was afraid everyone had run away.

But Paul and Silas called, "We are all here."
The jailer could hardly believe it.
He asked Paul and Silas what to do.
"Believe in Jesus," they told him.
And he did believe.
He let Paul and Silas out of jail.
Then he and his family were baptized.
And their hearts were full of joy and love.

For more information on
The Beginners Bible™
products, books or kids'
club, clearly print your
name, address and phone
number and send it to the
address below.

Attn: Brand Manager
Performance Unlimited, Inc
P.O. Box 3548
Brentwood, TN 37024

Look for the many fun products featuring the friendly characters from The Beginners Bible™

- Home Schooling Books
- Activity and Coloring Books
- Treasury of Bible Stories Gold Leaf Edition
- Sound Books
- Pop Up Books
- Dinnerware
- Videos
- Gift Cards
- Cassettes and CD's
- Educational Software
- Games
- Bedding and Wall Borders
- Collectible Figurines
- Stuffed Animals, Toys and more!

The Door into Heaven

John was one of Jesus' best friends.
He told many people about Jesus.
People began to follow Jesus' way.
The leaders did not like this.
They sent John away to an island
so he could not tell anyone about Jesus.

A New Heaven, *Revelation 1-22*

One day John heard a voice behind him.
It was loud like a trumpet.
John turned around.
He saw Jesus, shining like the sun.
"Do not be afraid," said Jesus.
"Write about what you see."

Then John saw an open door in heaven.
He saw God's throne
with a rainbow around it.
All day and night, creatures with wings kept
saying, "Holy, holy, holy is the Lord God
Almighty, who was and is and is to come."
John saw what was going to happen.
He saw the devil and his helpers
being thrown into a lake of fire.

He saw a new Heaven and a new earth.
He saw a new city of God.
A loud voice said, "God's people
will live with God now.
They will not need the sun or moon.
God's glory will give them light.
There will be no more dying
or crying or hurting.
God's people will live with Him
for ever and ever."
Then Jesus said, "I am coming soon."
And John said, "YES, JESUS, COME."